Smelly Crayons

AuthorHouse™
1663 Liberty Drive
Bloomington, IN 47403
www.authorhouse.com
Phone: 1 (800) 839-8640

This book is printed on acid-free paper.

ISBN: 978-1-5462-7380-6 (sc)
ISBN: 978-1-5462-7381-3 (e)

Print information available on the last page.

Published by AuthorHouse 05/07/2020

authorHOUSE®

Smelly Crayons

Anna Drew & Brittany Hillis

Illustrated by: Olsie Tula

One day after Brittany has done all her chores, mom promised her she would take her to the store to buy her new crayons and a coloring book. She picked the brightest crayons she could find and an all seasons coloring book.

Brittany opened the new crayons. She took the paper off each crayon, threw away the box, and place them in her purple case.

She opened her coloring book. She liked the little bunny marshmallows. She takes out her pick crayon and begins to color. She took a good whiff of the crayon she just colored and noticed that the crayon had a different smell than her other crayons.

She says, "Mom smell this."

She puts my nose up to the page. Mom says, "Mm, the color smells good, what does it smell like?"

Brittany shrugged her shoulders and said, "I don't know."

Suddenly, she snapped her fingers!
A light bulb flashed over her head.

She smiles and says all happy, "I
know, I know! Hot pick bubblegum!"

Mom asked, "Brittany would you like to help me write a story about your crayons?"

She answered, "Ok, I like that idea. The name of the book can be smelly crayons."

Mom said, "I love the title. Tell you what we can do. You make up the different names of the smelly crayons and will write them down. When we are finished, the story will be written."

She said, "That sounds good to me. I just can't wait. I better get busy thinking of good names. Mom I'm glad you are helping me, 'cause I'm 6 yrs. old and I don't think anyone would believe I wrote this by myself. Now would they?"

Mom laughed and reassured her that she would help Brittany write her story.

Brittany replied, "I better get busy and get back to work."

She walked back into her room. She took out her notebook and a pencil, she gave it to her mom and said, "Here is paper and pencil. You are going to need this. I will take care of the rest. Thanks mom."

Brittany flipped through the pages. She saw a thanksgiving scene of a thanksgiving feast with pilgrims and Indians.

She took out her brown crayon and began to color a bowl of nuts. She loved to eat nuts.

She smelled the picture, she thought to herself; *this crayon smells like a nut.*

She began to laugh. She brought out her coloring book and said while still laughing, "Mom smell this page, doesn't it smell like a nut?"

Mom replied, "Yes it does, the nuts in the picture are walnuts. I hope that helps."

"Thanks, Mom. That did help me."

She thought long and hard. Suddenly, she snapped her fingers, a lightbulb flashed over her head. She says, "I know, I know! Nutty brown."

She quickly ran to her mom and said, "Quick write this one down, Nutty brown."

Mom said, "I like the name, keep up the good work."

She yelled on the way back to her room "I will."

Brittany took out her bright yellow crayon. She flipped through the pages and saw a girl with very long hair.

She colored the girl hair bright yellow. She took a good whiff, she thought it smelled like lemons.

She went to her mom and asked, "Mom do you have any lemons?"

Mom answered, "Yes, I have lemons. Why do you ask?"

"I colored this girl's long hair yellow like mine. I took a good whiff and it smells like lemons. So now I asked because I would like some lemonade please."

She didn't have to think long and hard on this one. This one was the easiest one so far. She kept thinking...

Suddenly, she snapped her fingers. A lightbulb flashed over her head.

She said, "I know, I know! Little lemons" That was all she could come with.

She ran into the kitchen "Mom hurry write this one down." Mom quickly wrote it down.

She ran back to her room saying, "There are more names coming. Be ready!"

Brittany flipped through the pages. She saw a boy and girl running in a tall grass. She took out her green crayon.

She began to color the tall green grass. She took a good whiff.

The page smelled like grass. Brittany loved the smell of fresh cut grass.

Suddenly, she snapped her fingers, a lightbulb flashed over her head and said, "I know, I know, fresh cut green grass."

She ran to the kitchen. "Mom quick write this down. This one is the best one. Fresh cut green grass."

Mom replied, "Another great name. Good job."

She ran back to her room, saying "I will be back for more. Be ready."

She flipped through the pages. She colored a girl pretty flower dress red.

She came out to the kitchen and noticed fresh flowers on the table were the same flowers that were on the girl's dress.

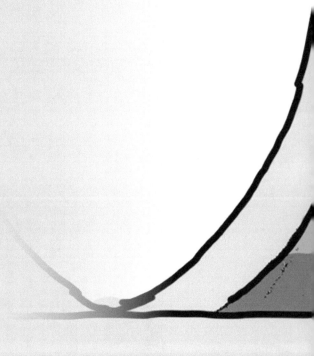
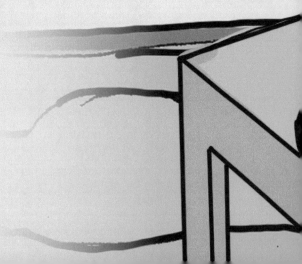

She asked, "Mom what kind of flowers are these that smell so good?"

"They are Roses," Mom replied.

Suddenly, she snapped her fingers and a lightbulb flashed over her head.

She smiles and said, "I know, I know! Red roses! Quick write this name down."

Mom thought it was another great name.

Brittany said, as she ran back to her room. "I will be back for more names. Have pen and paper ready!"

Brittany picked up a purple crayon. She wanted to know what it smelled like before she chose a page to color.

She scribbled on the inside of the coloring book. She took a good whiff. "Mm this smells like grapes."

She flipped through the pages until she came across the thanksgiving scene.

There was a bowl of what looked to be grapes. She colored it.

Suddenly, she snapped her fingers. A lightbulb flashed over her head. She smiled and said, "I know, fruity grape.

Mom quick write this one, Fruity grapes"

Mom quickly wrote it down.

"I really enjoyed coming up with names for the smelly crayons today, Mom!" exclaimed Brittany.

"You did a great job naming all of them," Mom replied.

"I still have a couple of colors left in the box that I haven't smelled yet. But I guess I need to let my nose rest for just a little bit. What do you think, Mom?"

"I sure will agree to that, Brittany. You better get your nose rested before you become a sniffing fox!"

TH END

(FOR NOW)

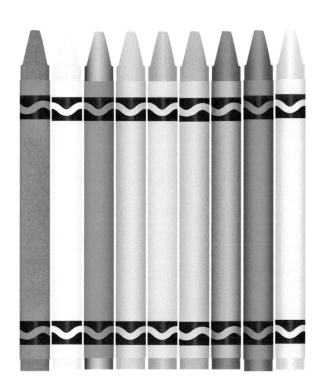

Printed in the United States
By Bookmasters